SELF-DECEPTION

SELF-DECEPTION

Its Nature, Evils, and Remedy

JACOB HELFFENSTEIN

Be not deceived.—GALATIANS 6:7.
Examine yourselves whether ye be in the faith.—2 CORINTHIANS 13:5.

CURIOSMITH

MINNEAPOLIS

Published by Curiosmith.
Minneapolis, Minnesota.
Internet: curiosmith.com.

Previously published by the AMERICAN TRACT SOCIETY in 1864.

The "Guide to the Contents" was added to this edition by the publisher.

ISBN 9781941281567

GUIDE TO THE CONTENTS

PREFACE

This little volume is affectionately commended to the serious perusal of every one bound to eternity, and especially of every professor of religion. It addresses them on a subject of infinite moment, involving their highest interest both for this world and the next. The writer would not excite the least unnecessary distrust or pain in a single bosom. He is well aware that there is a weak as well as a strong faith—that there are "babes" as well as "fathers" in Christ. The day of small things is not to be despised—the weak, timid believer is not to be crushed, but cherished and strengthened; yet it is better that the truth be faithfully exhibited, even though it should excite a momentary pang in the fearful, than to suffer multitudes who are trusting to "refuges of lies," to live and die unwarned. Reader, lay not this work aside until the great subject of which it treats is settled as you will wish it had been when your head is laid on the pillow of death, and the realities of eternity open upon your vision.

Chapter 1

THE NATURE AND FORMS OF SELF-DECEPTION

Self-deception may be distinguished from hypocrisy. The former consists in a wrong judgment of our character; the latter, in assuming one which we are conscious we do not possess, with the view of imposing upon our fellow-men, and accomplishing some sinister design. With such gross dissimulation the reader may not be chargeable. The very name of hypocrite may be regarded by him with abhorrence. All his professions may be characterized by the utmost sincerity.

But though he may not intentionally deceive others, he may fatally deceive himself. "There is a way which *seemeth* right unto a man; but the end thereof are the ways of death."[1] Sincerity affords no conclusive evidence of piety. A man may be sincere in the belief of error, as well as in the belief of truth—sincere in doing wrong, as well as in doing right. Paul "verily thought that he ought to do many

1 Proverbs 14:12.

things contrary to the name of Jesus of Nazareth."[1]

In the church of God there have ever been two classes of false professors. The one includes those, who, in the common acceptation of the term, are hypocrites[2]—those who, while they profess piety, are conscious they do not possess it; the other, those who view themselves as in a state of grace, when in fact they are in a state of nature—of sin and condemnation.

Nothing is more common, and certainly nothing more fatal than self-deception. The number who are ruined by false views of religion is doubtless great even when compared with those who perish in avowed infidelity or careless indifference. And as it is an act of kindness not less than an imperious duty to expose the delusions into which our fellow-men are liable to fall, we shall here endeavor to point out some of the modes in which the soul may be

1 Acts 26:9.

2 In the Scriptures, the term hypocrite seems to possess a meaning somewhat different from that which is usually attached to it. Here it is applied not simply to the *dissembler,* or the man who assumes a character which he knows does not belong to him, but to the *false professor.* Hence we find it appropriated to the Pharisees, who, as a people, appear to have been remarkably sincere, while at the same time they were charged with being "full of all uncleanness." Matthew 23. To this sect Saul of Tarsus belonged; and so devoted was he to the religion he professed, that he regarded himself "as, touching the righteousness of the law, blameless." (This is an original text footnote.)

deceived in the judgment it forms of its spiritual state and eternal prospects.

1. Many are deceived by mistaking the mere *dictates of the understanding* for the *gracious affections of the heart.*

This class of persons may be distinguished by the correctness of their sentiments and their opposition to error. Early instructed in the principles of Christianity, their minds have become stored with evangelical truth, and they will, perhaps, even "contend earnestly for the faith once delivered to the saints."[1]

The doctrines of entire depravity, of a vicarious atonement, of justification by faith, of regeneration by the Holy Spirit, and of an eternal state of retribution, have their unqualified assent, and constitute most essential articles in their creed. It may be that their speculative acquaintance with these doctrines is superior to that of many humble believers, and instances are not wanting in which unsanctified men have written in defense of those doctrines with great ability and effect.

Now it is easy to conceive how such persons may mistake a mere intellectual conviction of the truth for holiness of heart, especially if with an orthodox creed there be connected morality of life and a strict attention to the forms of godliness. The truth, however, <u>may be</u> *seen*, and yet not *loved*. The head may

1 Jude 1:3.

be filled with light, while the heart remains chilled with spiritual death. Such is the case with the fallen angels. They both know and believe the truth.

There may be also an *intellectual approbation of the truth* where its sanctifying power is wholly unknown. The manifestation which God has made of himself in creation has sometimes called forth expressions of the highest admiration, while the heart has shown itself to be in a state of decided enmity against his character. It is related of a lecturer on philosophy that, in discoursing on the wisdom and power of God as displayed in the immensity of creation, he with his audience was wrought up into a rapture of apparent devotion, and yet in less than an hour's time after leaving the room, he was heard to curse and swear, as was his usual manner of conversation.

Another common defect in that class of persons whose delusion we are now exposing, is, that while they *see* the truth they are not *affected* by it. It is contemplated simply in the abstract, without any reference to its bearing upon themselves. Theology is studied as a science, and the head becomes filled with ideas, while the affections remain cold and unmoved. They know that God is a being of infinite perfection, but do not love him; that sin is an infinite evil, but do not hate it; that Christ is supremely glorious, but do not esteem him; that there is a heaven, but are not allured by it—a hell, but do not fear it. True religion respects not simply the understanding, but the heart; it requires *love* as well as *light;* feeling—deep, ardent feeling. "John the Baptist was a 'burning and shining light.' To shine is not enough, a *glow-worm* will do so; to burn is not enough, a *fire-brand* will do so. Light without heat does but little good; and heat without light does much harm. Give me those Christians who are burning lamps as well as shining lights."[1]

Further, the truth may be *known* and yet not *obeyed*. It is one thing to know that repentance is a duty, another, to exercise repentance; one thing to know that faith in Christ is indispensable, another, actually to confide in him as the hope of the lost; one thing to know that "men ought always to pray," another, to "stir up ourselves to take hold on God." Religion is not mere speculation; it is obedience. "If ye know these things, happy are ye, if ye do them."[2] "To him that knoweth to do good, and doeth it not, to him it is sin."[3]

2. *Humanity* is often mistaken for *Christian benevolence.*

Total as is the apostasy of man, there still remain in him certain feelings of kindness and sympathy, which may attach to him a high degree of amiableness, and which answer important purposes in the

---

1 A quote from *The Nonsuch Professor* by William Secker.
2 John 13:17.
3 James 4:17.

present state of existence. To be "without natural affection" is represented by the apostle as the very climax of human depravity. Destitute as man is of love to God, there is notwithstanding a strong tendency in his nature "to weep with those that weep, and rejoice with those that rejoice"[1]—to pity the miserable, and to relieve the needy. This sympathetic feeling is often regarded as proof of moral goodness, when, in fact, it may exist where there is an entire alienation from God. The feeling is simply constitutional or instinctive. It exists in irrational animals as well as in man. The former, it is well known, are often deeply affected in view of their suffering offspring, and to preserve *them* will even sacrifice themselves.

Nothing is more common than for persons to commiserate the *temporal* calamities of others, while they manifest the most reckless disregard to their spiritual interests. We have seen the fond mother excited with intense emotion at the sight of an afflicted child, while that mother had no heart to feel for the soul of her offspring, exposed to eternal death, or to offer up one prayer to God for its redemption. We have seen men denominated philanthropists, prompt in lending their aid for the amelioration of human suffering, and yet not merely indifferent to the spiritual condition of the world, but actually hostile to that very Gospel

1 See Romans 12:15.

which constitutes the only balm for the woes which sin has entailed upon our race. Even "the tender mercies of the wicked are cruel."

3. Others are deceived by substituting *mere animal excitement* for holy *emotion*.

All our mental exercises produce more or less effect upon the body or the natural affections. It is not to be wondered at therefore that high religious emotions should sometimes overpower the animal frame. When Daniel had a view of the glory of Christ, there remained no strength in him. And John, speaking of a similar manifestation, says, "when I saw him I fell at his feet as dead."[1] Such affections, however, afford no evidence either of the genuineness or the spuriousness of our religion. They are merely *natural* effects, evincing indeed a high degree of mental excitement without determining whether that excitement be produced by the agency of the Spirit, or whether it be a fire of our own kindling. No dependence, therefore, can be placed upon such appearances themselves as a test of our own piety or the piety of others. Men may be melted to tears, groan in anguish, tremble with fear, or be transported with joy, while the natural sympathies merely are excited, and the heart remains unchanged.

4. *Remorse* is often mistaken for *repentance.*

Remorse is that mental pain or anguish which

1 Revelation 1:17.

is produced by a sense of guilt. This is widely different from true repentance; nor is there any necessary connection between the two. Cain, Pharaoh, Belshazzar, Judas, and thousands more whose sins found them out, and who were made to tremble in view of their consequences, remained entire strangers to the tenderness of contrition.

Perhaps the time was when the reader, like Gallio, "cared for none of these things." The subject of religion, if not treated with open contempt, was at least treated with criminal indifference. Instead of asking, "What must I do to be saved?" your incessant inquiry was, "What shall I eat, what shall I drink, or wherewithal shall I be clothed?" It is not so now. Your slumber has been broken. Light has been reflected upon your path; sin has revived; the world has lost its charms; and the salvation of the soul appears as "the one thing needful."

This change is certainly desirable. The sinner must be convicted before he can be converted; and yet no degree of conviction is evidence of conversion. The understanding may be enlightened and yet the heart maintain its rebellion. Conscience may be aroused, and yet not pacified by "the blood of sprinkling." Sin may be revealed, and yet not renounced. Obligation may be felt, and yet resisted. Conviction produces no change of character. It is light, but not holiness. It makes the sinner feel that he is lost, but does not necessarily secure his salvation. In the judgment of the great day, men will be overwhelmed with conviction, but there will be no repentance. In hell there will be conviction, deep and eternal conviction, but there will be no contrition—no pardon—no hope.

5. Many confound *selfish with holy affections.*

It is not enough that the affections be moved on the subject of religion; they must be moved aright. It is not the *degree* of feeling we possess that determines our character, but the *nature* of that feeling. Under a conviction of the immense value of the soul and the fearful consequences of impenitence, the mind may be burdened with solicitude while sin still maintains its sway. "Let me die," said Balaam, "the death of the righteous, and let my last end be like his."[1]

Unregenerate men may be as much excited on the subject of religion as true Christians, but the nature of the excitement differs essentially. The Israelites at the Red Sea appeared greatly affected with gratitude to God for their deliverance, but they soon "forgat his works" and rebelled against his dispensations. While the Savior was upon earth, going about doing good, many followed him for a time, not from a regard to his person and doctrine, but "for the loaves and fishes."

We are far from intimating that men should have no "respect to the recompense of reward"; but

1 Numbers 23:10.

we maintain that God must be the *supreme* object of our affection, and that he must be loved not simply for the favors he has conferred upon us, but for his own intrinsic excellency. "If ye love them which love you, what reward have ye? do not even publicans the same?"[1] An important distinction has been made between self-love and selfishness. The former consists in a proper regard to our own happiness. This principle is implanted in man by the Creator himself, and its operation is consistent with the highest degree of holiness. Selfishness is the inordinate love of our personal happiness, regardless both of the glory of God and the interests of our fellow-beings. This constitutes the very essence of sin, and, of course, no degree in which it is exercised, nor any modification it may assume, can afford evidence of a holy character. Men may be as supremely selfish in religion as they are in the world.

6. Others are deceived by taking *reformation* for *regeneration*.

A good man out of the good treasure of his heart will indeed bring forth good things. His character will be determined by his conduct. The heart is no better than the life. If the fountain be pure, the streams will be so too. In vain however do we attempt to cleanse the streams while the fountain remains corrupt. Such was the case with the Pharisees. Our Savior appropriately compares them

1 Matthew 5:46.

with "whited sepulchres," which, however beautiful they may be without, are "within full of all uncleanness."

It is no uncommon thing for one form of sin to be exchanged for another. A man may abandon a course of open profligacy only to settle down upon a system of self-righteousness. We read of those who "turn to the Lord feignedly, but not with their whole heart."[1]

Nothing short of a *radical* change can constitute us Christians. Man by nature is not *partially* but *entirely* depraved. It is not enough therefore to *do better*. This would suppose the existence of some previous goodness; whereas regeneration is the *beginning* of holiness. The change, moreover, respects not merely the life, but the heart. It does not consist in improving any principle of holiness already existing, but in exercising the first holy affection.

In the present day of reforms, peculiar caution is necessary lest a mere renunciation of certain vices be substituted for the "renewing of the Holy Ghost." The temperance cause has done much to modify human conduct as well as to ameliorate human misery. It has often too proved a pioneer to religion. We can heartily bid it "God-speed," and can most earnestly pray for its final triumph; and yet it must not be concealed that to become sober is

1 See Jeremiah 3:10.

no proof, that we have become Christians.

7. *The form* of godliness is often assumed where *its power* is absent.

By the *form*, we understand the observance of the mere externals of religion; by the *power*, the practical influence of religion upon the heart and the life—dominion over sin, a sense of pardon, communion with God, the spirit of prayer, patience under suffering, victory over death, and the joyful hope of a blessed immortality. Now, though the power of religion can hardly exist without the form, the form may and often does exist without the power. Profession is not possession. The picture of a man is not a man. It may have a strong resemblance, but it wants the most essential part—vitality. We may have "a name to live," and yet be spiritually dead— may call Jesus "Lord," and yet practically disregard his authority—may sing with the lip, and yet make no "melody in the heart"—may bow the knee to God in prayer, and yet never prostrate ourselves before him in spirit—may appear among the guests at the Lord's Supper, and yet, instead of being clad with the "wedding garment," come with a dress of our own.

No class of men were ever more regular in their observance of the rites and ceremonies of religion than the Pharisees. They fasted twice in the week, and gave tithes of all that they possessed—they made broad their phylacteries, and enlarged the borders of their garments; and yet all their external sanctity was but a cloak to hide the deep depravity of the heart.

Other motives than those derived from the influence of the Gospel may secure attention to the forms of religion. Early education, a regard to their standing in society, or the goadings of an awakened conscience, have induced multitudes to abound in such observances when the heart has been far from God. Mr. Whitefield, in speaking of his state previous to his conversion, remarks: "When I was sixteen years of age I began to fast twice a week for thirty-six hours together, prayed many times a day, received the sacrament every Lord's day, fasting myself almost to death all the forty days of Lent, during which I made it a point of duty never to go less than three times a day to public worship, besides seven times a day to my private prayers, yet I knew no more that I was to be born again in God, born a new creature in Christ Jesus, than if I had never been born at all."

8. *Gifts* are often mistaken for *graces*.

Many have regarded themselves as eminent Christians from the circumstance of their being fluent in prayer, talented in conversation, eloquent in address, or distinguished for their attainments in biblical knowledge. The most splendid talents, however, may be connected with an unsanctified heart. Saul had the spirit of prophecy, and Judas probably wrought miracles. The language of the apostle clearly implies that a man may speak with the tongues of men and angels, may have the gift of prophecy, and understand all mysteries and all knowledge, may have all faith, so that he could remove mountains, may bestow all his goods to feed the poor, and give his body to be burned, and yet be destitute of that charity without which all our attainments and performances are but "as sounding brass and a tinkling cymbal."[1]

Men may be endowed with talents by which they may be rendered highly useful to others, while they become "cast-aways" themselves. They may preach the Gospel with discrimination, and even with success, while that Gospel exerts no sanctifying influence upon their own hearts. They may guide others to heaven, and in the end be excluded themselves. "There were builders of the ark whose floating corpses were sunk beneath it when it rose upon the bosom of the flood. There were donors of the tabernacle who were as lepers thrust beyond the camp, or as blasphemers stoned without relief. There were artificers of the temple who never there left their offerings, and never there worshipped God."

9. *Sectarian attachment and party zeal* are often mistaken for *Christian devotedness*.

The Pharisees, with all their aversion to true

---

1 1 Corinthians 13:1–3.

piety, "compassed sea and land to make one proselyte." The zeal of papists in the propagation of error has often exceeded that of Protestants in the propagation of truth. There are sects noted for their fanaticism and delusion, whose efforts to gain converts could hardly be surpassed by the most devoted and self-denying Christians. Those who are strangers to piety may no doubt be as full of zeal as those who are under its influence, while the motives by which they are governed may differ essentially. It is possible for men to preach, to write, to pray, and to suffer for what they deem the cause of truth, when in fact they are influenced by no higher aim than a desire to promote the interests of a party. With all their apparent devotedness they may look with indifference upon the evident good effected in other branches of Zion. Instead of rejoicing in the success of other evangelical denominations, it may give them pain. While a revival of religion among themselves may be extolled as a wonderful work of God, the same favorable appearances exhibited among Christians of a different name may beget feelings of envy and jealousy.

Will the reader here pause, and carefully inquire on what ground he is resting his hope of future happiness? Beware of trusting to a "refuge of lies." Dig deep, and lay the foundation low. The day of trial is hastening on, and every fabric not built upon the Rock must totter and fall. "All is not gold that glitters." There may be the *appearance* of piety where there is not the *reality*. Rest, then, upon nothing that will not bear examination, and that will not endure the coming storm. It is not enough that you have a hope; see that you have "a good hope, through grace."

Chapter 2

THE DANGER OF SELF-DECEPTION

In the former chapter we pointed out some of the innumerable methods of self-deception; in the present we purpose to show our extreme liability to the evil.

1. We are liable to self-deception *from the state of our own hearts.*

These are "deceitful above all things." There is no knowledge of more importance, and yet none more difficult to acquire, than the knowledge of ourselves. The greatest obstacle to its attainment lies in the natural pride and treachery of the heart. We are prone to think more highly of ourselves than we ought to think, to regard our character with complacency, and to put the most favorable construction upon our conduct. The very idea of being under the wrath of God is so exceedingly repulsive to all our feelings, that it is admitted with extreme reluctance, and not until the evidence of the fact can no longer be resisted. If we own that our condition is bad, we suppose it might be worse. Whatever may be our blemishes, we fancy they are more than made up by our virtues.

The depravity of the heart blinds the understanding so that we call evil good, and good evil, light darkness, and darkness light. We are naturally averse to self-examination, and when we attempt it we are disposed to judge ourselves by a wrong standard. Many things are taken for evidences of piety which are not such in reality. While we carefully seize upon every thing which presents itself in our favor, our deficiencies are overlooked, or regarded as of little moment. "The way of the wicked is as darkness, they know not at what they stumble."[1]

2. We are not only liable to self-deception from the depravity of the heart, *Satan, too, exerts a powerful influence in promoting the same object.*

"As a roaring lion he walketh about seeking whom he may devour."[2] And it is evident that the means which he employs to accomplish his designs are characterized by the profoundest *artifice.* Hence we read of his "wiles"—his "snare"—his "devices." He "blinds the minds of them which believe not, lest the light of the glorious Gospel of Christ, who is the image of God, should shine unto them."[3] He even "transforms himself into an angel of light,"

---

1 Proverbs 4:19.

2 1 Peter 5:8.

3 2 Corinthians 4:4.

representing truth as error, and error as truth, holiness as sin, and sin as holiness. He has temptations adapted to every mind, and to every condition. If one means fail, he can employ another. If one form of self-deception will not answer his purpose, a thousand more are at hand.

First of all, perhaps, he diverts the attention of the sinner altogether from the subject of religion, prejudices him against its claims, occupies him with the world, or tempts him to presume on future repentance. But if, in spite of such efforts, conscience becomes alarmed, the next step may be to lead the inquirer to the indulgence of a false hope. By suggesting some promise of the Bible, by misrepresenting the character of God, or by counterfeiting the evidences of piety, the great adversary often succeeds in quieting every fear, and lulling the soul into a sleep more profound than that from which it had been aroused. He "taketh with himself seven other spirits more wicked than himself, and they enter in and dwell there; and the last state of that man is worse than the first."[1]

3. The danger of self-deception will also appear from *the frequent distinction which the Bible makes between true and false religion.*

Is there a *"love* which is the fulfilling of the law?" there is also a love entirely selfish, and which in times of temptation "waxes cold." Is there a *"godly*

1 Matthew 12:45.

sorrow which worketh repentance unto salvation?" there is also a "sorrow of the world, which worketh death." Is there a *faith* which "worketh by love" and "overcometh the world?" there is also a faith dead and inoperative. Is there a *filial fear* which is "the beginning of wisdom?" there is also a slavish fear, which often agitates the wicked on earth, and which will be to them a source of torment for ever. It is said of the Samaritans that "they feared the Lord *and* served their own gods."[1] Is there a *submission* which results from enlightened views of the Divine government and a cordial approbation of the Divine dispensations? there is also a submission feigned and forced. "Through the greatness of thy power," says the Psalmist, "shall thine enemies submit themselves unto thee."[2] Is there "a *good hope* through grace" which "purifieth the heart," and proves "as an anchor of the soul, both sure and steadfast?" there is also a hope which maketh ashamed—the "hope of the hypocrite," which "shall be as the giving up of the ghost." Is there a *joy* which is "sown for the righteous," and which is the "fruit of the Spirit?" there is also the joy of the stony-ground hearers, who having "no root in them," soon wither under the influence of persecution and trial.

Thus it appears that every Christian grace has

1 2 Kings 17:33; Zephaniah 1:5.
2 Psalm 66:3.

its counterfeits. The question, then, is not simply whether we have love to God, sorrow for sin, faith in Christ, submission, fear, hope and joy—but what is the nature of these exercises? Are they such as God requires—such as are peculiar to the saints—such as will be approved in the great day of final retribution?

4. *The admonitions and warnings of the Bible* afford another evidence of the danger of self-deception.

"Let no man deceive himself."[1] "Let every man prove his own work."[2] "Examine yourselves whether ye be in the faith; prove your own selves."[3] "Be ye doers of the word, and not hearers only, deceiving your own selves."[4] "Let us fear lest a promise being left us of entering into his rest, any of you should seem to come short of it."[5] "Looking diligently, lest any man fail of the grace of God."[6]

Now consider to *whom* these injunctions were originally directed. They were addressed to professors of religion, who had exhibited credible evidence of piety, and who had endured the severest trials in their adherence to the truth. And if such needed to be cautioned against self-delusion, then let none,

1 1 Corinthians 3:18.
2 Galatians 6:4.
3 2 Corinthians 13:5.
4 James 1:22.
5 Hebrews 4:1.
6 Hebrews 12:15.

at the present day, flatter themselves that they are secure. The highest attainments in the divine life are consistent with the closest self-examination, and the most incessant watchfulness over our own hearts. While we stand we have need to take heed lest we fall. "Search me," said the Psalmist, "O God, and know my heart; try me, and know my thoughts; and see if there be any wicked way in me, and lead me in the way everlasting."[1] "I keep under my body," says Paul, "and bring it into subjection, lest that by any means, when I have preached to others, I myself should be a cast-away."[2]

5. The Scriptures not only teach us that men may be deceived, *but that many actually are deceived.*

Instances of this kind abound in the word of God for the instruction and warning of others in every subsequent age. We read of those, who, when they hear the words of the curse, bless themselves in their heart, saying, "I shall have peace though I walk in the imagination of mine heart";[3] of those who "flatter themselves in their own eyes until their iniquity be found to be hateful";[4] of those who are "pure in their own eyes, and yet are not washed from their filthiness";[5] of those who cry "Peace and

1 Psalm 139:23, 24.
2 1 Corinthians 9:27.
3 Deuteronomy 29:19.
4 Psalms 36:2.
5 Proverbs 30:12.

safety" when "sudden destruction" awaits them;[1] of those who say that they are "rich and increased with goods, and have need of nothing, and know not that they are wretched, and miserable, and poor, and blind, and naked."[2] As a nation, the Jews in the days of Christ were under the influence of the most fatal self-delusion. While they boasted of their pious ancestry, and of their distinguished privileges, and regarded themselves as the exclusive objects of divine favor, the Savior, who saw through every disguise, declared that the love of God was not in them.[3]

Even in the *Christian* church there were some, who, while they professed to know God, "in works denied him"—who called themselves the friends of Christ, but walked as the enemies of his cross— who maintained the form of godliness but denied its power. What characters are denoted by the five foolish virgins but members of the visible church, bearing indeed the lamp of profession but utterly void of divine grace. Who is the man without a "wedding garment," but one who finds his way within the pale of the church, and takes his place at the communion-table, and yet, instead of being clothed with the "garment of salvation," appears in the "filthy rags" of his own righteousness.

1 See 1 Thessalonians 5:3.
2 Revelation 3:17.
3 See John 5:42.

Among the twelve apostles there was a traitor. Among the thousands numbered as converts during the great revival which commenced on the day of Pentecost, there were an Ananias and a Sapphira.

And if cases of self-deception existed in the primitive church, to which none were admitted who did not afford credible evidence of evangelical repentance and faith, what must be the state of a church where a profession of vital godliness is not regarded as essential to membership? If the tares grew among the wheat when special pains were taken to prevent their introduction, what may we not look for where the two are knowingly mingled together? Notwithstanding the utmost precaution in the reception of persons to "sealing ordinances," individuals will still "creep in unawares," who, instead of belonging to the "household of faith," belong to the world.

In almost every church, however pure, are perhaps some whom "a deceived heart hath turned aside." Such professors may maintain a good and regular standing for years; their attendance on the ordinances of God's house may be constant and punctual, and their piety beyond all suspicion, and yet when weighed in the balances they may be found wanting. Legh Richmond, according to his own testimony, had not only been a member of the church, but had also entered upon the Christian ministry before he became savingly acquainted with the truth as it is in Jesus.

Religious biography furnishes us with numerous instances in which persons have experienced great changes in their views and feelings, while they have remained ignorant of that one great change which the Scriptures declare to be essential to salvation.

President Edwards, when a small boy, was greatly excited about his salvation; had very clear views of his lost and guilty state; wept and prayed much with deep feeling; obtained, as he thought, pardon for his sins, and felt very happy and joyful afterwards. For a time he loved to pray and talk about religion, and he united with other boys and held a youth's prayer-meeting. After a while all these feelings left him, and he became a thoughtless, stupid young man. Again he was awakened, deeply convicted for sin, and again obtained peace and joy; but he describes this second experience as essentially different from the first, in that he obtained scriptural views of Christ as his justifying righteousness, and his views of God and holiness were entirely different. This double conversion, so to speak, qualified him with superior light in the Scriptures to write with uncommon discrimination upon religious experience. *"Edwards on the Affections"* is a book that should be read carefully and frequently by professors of religion.

David Brainerd passed through a similar false experience, and really thought he had religion; but afterwards learned his mistake, and became truly converted, and lived a life of eminent piety and spirituality till his death.

The late Andrew Fuller, one of the most distinguished theological writers of the age, was the subject of conviction of sin from childhood. He was often much affected while thinking upon the doctrines of Christianity. At the age of 13 years he rested upon a *false hope*, from having these words *suddenly* impressed upon his mind: "Sin shall not have dominion over you; for ye are not under the law, but under grace."[1] This filled him with joy and transport; and he seemed, to use his own language, "as in a new world. It appeared to me I hated all my sins and was resolved to forsake them." But notwithstanding all this, in a few days he cast off serious impressions and went headlong into sin, and for a time he used to think himself a backsliding Christian, though in a little time, as he says, his conscience almost became seared. He was afterwards truly converted.

Here is the spot where hundreds fail. They take up with a conversion that falls infinitely short of saving faith in Jesus Christ, and when they lose their religious impressions, and live habitually in the neglect of secret and family prayer and other religious duties, they lay the flattering unction to their consciences that they are backsliding saints,

1 See Romans 6:15.

and that God will bring them back in his own good time.

6. What must tend to impress our minds still more deeply with the danger of self-deception, is *the fact that multitudes not only live but die deceived.*

A death-bed has indeed been called a "detector of the heart." Thus it has no doubt proved in numerous instances. The confidence which the deceived have cherished in health, has utterly failed on the near approach of eternity. "What is the hope of the hypocrite, though he hath gained, when God taketh away his soul?"[1]

We cannot, however, determine the safety of a person by the manner of his death. If men may *live* deceived, no reason can be given why they may not *die* deceived. It is recorded of the wicked that "there are no bands in their death." The former character of many who have departed this life in peace, furnishes fearful evidence that even in the honest hour of dissolution men may cling to a hope which will at last prove "like the spider's web." While Bunyan represents *Christian* and *Hopeful* as entering upon the river of death with hesitation and fear, the case of *Ignorance* (a character by no means rare) is described in the following affecting language.

"Now while I was gazing upon all these things, I turned my head to look back, and saw Ignorance come up to the river side; but he soon got over, and

1 Job 27:8.

without half the difficulty which the other two men met with. For it had happened that there was then in the place one Vain Hope, a ferryman, that with his boat helped him over; so he, as the others I saw, did ascend the hill, to come up to the gate; only he came alone; neither did any meet him with the least encouragement. When he was come up to the gate, he looked up to the writing that was above, and then began to knock, supposing that entrance should have been quickly administered to him; but he was asked by the men that looked over the top of the gate, Whence came you? and what would you have? He answered, I have ate and drank in the presence of the King, and he has taught in our streets. Then they asked him for his certificate, that they might go in and show it to the King. So he fumbled in his bosom for one and found none. Then said they, Have you none? but the man answered never a word. So they told the King, but he would not come down to see him, but commanded the two shining ones, that conducted Christian and Hopeful to the city, to go out and take Ignorance, and bind him hand and foot, and have him away. Then they took him up and carried him through the air to the door that I saw in the side of the hill, and put him in there. Then I saw that there was a way to hell, even from the gate of heaven as well as from the City of Destruction."

Chapter 3

THE CONSEQUENCES OF SELF-DECEPTION

Self-deception in religion is a terrific evil. Its disastrous influence both in this world and the next exceeds all description. Nothing can befall us this side eternity which should be more deprecated, and against which we should more carefully guard. A false hope is worse than no hope. Whatever distress may attend the latter, the former is by far the more ruinous.

1. Self-deception *renders all our religious performances vain.*

With whatever complacency they may be viewed by ourselves or by our fellow-men, infinite purity cannot behold them but with abhorrence. If the heart be wrong, all is wrong. Where there is no holy principle, there can be no holy practice. The same works that the Christian performs we may perform, and they may be performed, too, with the same apparent zeal; but if our motives be impure they destroy the moral virtue of our deeds, however splendid and imposing to the eye of man, and render them in the view of God nothing but "vain oblations."

Do we "spread forth our hands" in prayer? "He that turneth away his ear from hearing the law, even his prayer shall be abomination."[1] Do we appear in the sanctuary? "Who," says God, "hath required this at your hand to tread my courts?"[2] Do we pay an external respect to the Sabbath? "The new moons and Sabbaths, the calling of assemblies, I cannot away with: it is iniquity, even the solemn meeting."[3] Do we afflict ourselves by fasting? "Is it such a fast that I have chosen? a day for a man to afflict his soul? is it to bow down his head as a bulrush and to spread sackcloth and ashes under him? wilt thou call this a fast and an acceptable day to the Lord?"[4] Do we surround the Lord's table and receive the sacred memorials of the Savior's death? Instead of commemorating his sufferings we become "guilty of the body and blood of the Lord." Do we give of our substance to feed the poor or to support and extend the Gospel? Verily we have our reward, the praise of man, but not the approbation of God.

2. Self-deception also *deprives us of the present comforts of religion.*

It may indeed impart a certain kind of peace.

---

1 Proverbs 28:9.

2 Isaiah 1:12.

3 Isaiah 1:13.

4 Isaiah 58:5.

The mind, before agitated with fear, may become calmed, but to the "joy of salvation" we shall notwithstanding remark strangers. Religion, so far from proving a pleasure, will prove a task. Its duties will be observed, not because they are deemed desirable in themselves, but only as a means for the attainment of some selfish end.

3. Self-deception will *prevent us from deriving any benefit from the means of grace.*

Regarding our condition as already safe, we shall of course see no ground for alarm.

Whatever denunciations the Bible may utter against the impenitent, those denunciations will be lost upon us. Ministers may preach with the utmost fidelity, "warning every man with tears," "reproving, rebuking, exhorting with all long-suffering and doctrine," but the Gospel, instead of becoming to us "the savor of life unto life," will become "the savor of death unto death."

Do they urge their hearers to "flee from the wrath to come?" According to our apprehension, we have already been saved from that wrath. Do they point to "the Lamb of God who taketh away the sin of the world?" We have already looked to him as our Savior. Do they portray the glories of heaven, and call upon us to "lay hold on eternal life?" Heaven is already made sure. Do they caution us against self-delusion? Others may be deceived but as it respects ourselves, we cannot be mistaken.

It is comparatively easy to shake the hopes of some real Christians, while the same truths which disturb them leave the hypocrite unmoved. While some weak, trembling believer may lay this little volume aside, writing bitter things against himself, the very class of persons for whose benefit it is more immediately intended, may read its pages without one feeling of distrust or apprehension.

4. The dreadfulness of self-deception will further appear when we reflect that *in eternity it will be too late to rectify the mistake.*

Then indeed it will be manifest. A view of the holy character of God, and of the spirituality of his law, will at once dissipate every delusion. The heart will appear without a covering, and every form of self-delusion will vanish for ever; but there will be no remedy—probation has closed—the character is formed, and the record of our lives sealed up for eternity.

> No Patron! Intercessor none! now past
> The sweet, the clement, mediatorial hour!
> For guilt no plea! to pain no pause! no bound!
> Inexorable all! and all extreme![1]

5. Self-deception will also *aggravate our future misery.*

The more confident our hopes of future

---

[1] A quote from *Night Thoughts* by Edward Young.

happiness are here, the more bitter will be the pain of disappointment hereafter. How awful to go to the gate of heaven, expecting admission, and then meet the sentence, "Depart from me, all ye workers of iniquity!"[1] Imagination can form but little conception of the anguish which must follow this exclusion. "There shall be weeping and gnashing of teeth," says Jesus, "when ye shall see Abraham, and Isaac, and Jacob, and all the prophets in the kingdom of God, and you yourselves thrust out."[2] Picture to yourself the deceived professor on his death-bed. He fears no evil—even to the last he retains his confidence and remains calm. He dies, it may be, exulting in hope—but where is he? Instead of finding himself in heaven, he is in hell! Instead of mingling with the spirits of the blessed, he is associated with the lost! Instead of swelling the note of redemption to the Lamb, he mourns in despair that "the harvest is past, the summer ended, and he is not saved."[3]

O the darkness that must gather around the spirit when the light of hope is thus suddenly and for ever extinguished! The hope of the hypocrite, it is said, shall be "as the giving up of the Ghost"— like the separation of the soul from the body—as certain and as dreadful. "His hope shall be cut off,

1 Psalm 6:8.
2 Luke 13:27, 28.
3 Jeremiah 8:20.

and his trust shall be a spider's web. He shall lean upon his house; but it shall not stand; he shall hold it fast, but it shall not endure."[1] The fabric which he had all his life been rearing will fall, and great indeed will be the fall![2]

"To sink into hell from the table of the Lord! O, what a terrible fall! They that perished from Sodom and Gomorrah, though their punishment will be intolerable, will be but slightly punished in comparison with you. A lost communicant!—one that went to hell with the bread and wine, the memorials of a dying Savior, as it were in his mouth! O, I think such a one must be the most shocking sight in the infernal regions. How will lost angels and lost heathens wonder and stare at you as a horrible phenomenon, a dreadful curiosity! How will they upbraid you, 'How art thou fallen from heaven, O Lucifer, son of the morning, art thou also become as one of us?'"[3]

---

1 Job 8:14, 15.

2 See Matthew 7:27.

3 A quote from *The Christian Feast* a sermon by Samuel Davies.

Chapter 4

SELF-DECEPTION LIABLE TO PROVE PERMANENT

"They hold fast deceit, they refuse to return."[1] This solemn charge was brought against professors of religion. Notwithstanding the variety of means which had been employed to convince them of their danger and lead them to repentance, they continued to cleave to their delusions and proved utterly incorrigible. *There is an awful probability that the deceived professor of religion will remain deceived until probation closes, and all opportunity of salvation ceases for ever.* "All things," indeed, "are possible with God." He can work when, where, and upon whom he please. So far, however, as we are acquainted with the operations of his grace, they are but seldom extended to those who have taken up with a false profession and hope. The Scriptures speak of the conversion of thousands, but I do not recollect that they speak of the conversion of one, in the *Christian* church,

1 Jeremiah 8:5.

who had been deceived with a spurious piety.

"I believe," says Dr. Griffin, "there is no instance recorded in the Bible of a sinner's being rescued from a false hope unless it was founded in the belief of a false religion. In the short period which I have had to make my observations, I recollect very few instances of persons apparently renewed after they had settled down for years upon a false hope and with that hope had joined the church. Indeed, I remember but one. We read of tares, we read of foolish virgins, but we never read of their conversion."

Speaking of those who imagine themselves to be converted when they are not, President Edwards remarks that he had "scarcely known the instance of such an one in his life that had been undeceived." The confident hope of the hypocrite, he says, is "in one sense much more immoveable than truly gracious assurance."

The conversion of a false professor can be effected only by destroying his present confidence; but how reluctantly does he yield that confidence, especially where it has been long cherished and strengthened. In times of special revival, when God "searches Jerusalem with candles," "sinners in Zion" often become afraid; but in the ordinary state of feeling which prevails in the church, there is but little probability that they will renounce their hopes and become the subjects of renewing grace.

1. The *manner in which the Scriptures speak of*

the sense of security created by a false hope, is full of instruction and warning.

"What," says Job, "is the hope of the hypocrite though he hath gained, when God taketh away his soul?"[1] Here, the hypocrite's hope is represented as continuing *until death*, as though nothing but the separation of the soul from the body could separate him from his imagined security.

The Scriptures speak of such as flatter themselves in their own eyes until their iniquity be found to be hateful—hateful either in their conversion or perdition.[2]

They moreover teach us that men may continue the cry, "Peace and safety, until sudden destruction come upon them."[3]

Those who built on the sand are described as secure until "the rain descended, and the floods came, and the winds blew,"[4] and their edifice was utterly demolished.

The foolish virgins appeared as well satisfied with their condition as the wise. Nothing but the unexpected cry, "Behold, the Bridegroom cometh; go ye out to meet him," disturbed their repose and convinced them of their folly.[5]

---

1 Job 27:8.
2 See Psalm 36:2.
3 1 Thessalonians 5:3.
4 Matthew 7:27.
5 See Matthew 25:1–13.

2. Another consideration which renders it probable that deceived professors will remain deceived, is *the fact that their morality blinds them to their condition*.

No evangelical church can tolerate immorality in its members. As a moral life is regarded indispensable to their admission, so it is also requisite to their continuance. When churches become so corrupt as knowingly to receive and retain in fellowship those whose conduct is openly vicious, they can hardly be acknowledged as churches of Christ. Now, the fact that professors of religion are usually distinguished for the correctness of their conduct, presents a strong reason why those who are deceived may remain under that deception. Press upon the profligate the claims of the Gospel, and he will, perhaps, admit that he is not what he ought to be; but speak to an unconverted church-member on the subject, and he can effectually fortify himself against your appeals, by reference to his exemplary deportment.

The power of this delusion is usually strengthened where the individual once led an abandoned life and afterwards became reformed. How easy is it to mistake a change of conduct for a change of character! How prone are we to suppose that because we have lopped off some of the branches, we have struck at the root itself!

3. Again, *their connection with the visible*

church tends also to promote the confidence of the deceived.

Previous to this connection, regarding themselves as yet "of the world," they may have often felt seriously alarmed. They saw others approaching the sacramental supper while they were excluded, and the apprehension would sometimes arise that they might never sit down at "the marriage supper of the Lamb"; but their names are now enrolled among the people of God, and it is assumed that those names must be recorded in the "book of life." They have fled to the temple and grasped the horns of the altar, and feel themselves consequently to be secure. The shield of their profession effectually wards off every arrow of conviction. The shafts of divine justice fall harmless at their feet. Others may writhe under the power of truth, but they are invulnerable. "The temple of the Lord, the temple of the Lord, the temple of the Lord," say they, "are we."

4. Their *observance of the external duties of religion* increases their sense of security.

Perhaps they are distinguished not only for their regular appearance in the sanctuary on the Sabbath, but also for their attendance at the lecture and prayer-meeting during the week. It is possible, too, that they may have established an altar in their families, and may maintain a form of devotion in the closet. They may also be among the first to patronize the benevolent objects of the day, and to take an active part in every thing pertaining to the external prosperity of the church.

Now the tendency of all these observances, where there is a destitution of love to God or true piety, is to quiet conscience and fill the mind with self-complacency. When a man engages in such things with a proper spirit, his moral sensibility, instead of being diminished, is increased; but where they are attended to with a different spirit, they usually result in increased hardness of heart, and become as opiates to the soul. The sin of thus trifling with sacred truths and duties is one of peculiar aggravation, and on that account is visited with spiritual judgments. "Be not mockers," says God, "lest your bands be made strong."

The more an unregenerate professor is put forward in the affairs of the church, the more familiar he becomes with divine truth, and the more he abounds in external observances, the more, not unfrequently, is his danger enhanced, and the difficulties in the way of his conversion multiplied.

5. *The similarity between true and false experience* is another circumstance by which a delusive hope is strengthened.

A Christian relates the dealings of God with his soul. He speaks of his sense of sin, and his desert of condemnation. He speaks of the anguish which took hold on his spirit when the law laid upon him its claims and thundered against him its anathemas.

He speaks of his peace and joy in the Holy Ghost.

A false convert, in listening to the relation, imagines that he discerns a similarity between his own exercises and those of the believer. He, too, has been the subject of fear and of hope, of sorrow and of joy. He, too, has trembled in view of the coming wrath, and as he supposes, fled to Christ as his refuge. There is not a single exercise of grace which may not have its counterfeit. Men will speak in affecting terms of the delusion of the moralist and the Pharisee, and dream not of danger in their own case. They count themselves the friends of vital piety, and the subjects of evangelical experience; and should their neglect of duty or their want of devotedness to Christ excite suspicion that all is not right, reference to the circumstances of their supposed conversion will remove their apprehensions and restore their wonted confidence. To doubt the genuineness of their conversion they think an act of unbelief no less dishonorable to God than injurious to themselves.

6. *The favorable opinion which others entertain of their piety* also promotes their security.

Though "dead in trespasses and sins," they have "a name to live." Their standing in the church is good and regular. They are regarded as Christians and treated as such.

Perhaps their experience is not only judged to be satisfactory, but striking, and their charitable contributions and labors may be referred to as examples worthy of imitation. Why then should they doubt? Would they be regarded as Christians by men of such wisdom and piety, if they had no claim to the Christian character?

7. Farther—*they see others in the church live just as they live.*

Should their inconsistencies occasionally lead them to doubt their conversion, they find others whose conduct is in accordance with their own or whose piety is even far more dubious. "All," say they, "have their imperfections, and we have ours. The best men are but men at best—let him who is without sin cast the first stone." They are most keen to discern the Christian's blemishes, but alas, they entirely overlook his humiliation!

8. *Perhaps they have also seen some who lived as they live, die at last in peace.*

The hopes of the self-deceived, as we have already remarked, often remain firm even in death. Their end is calm and peaceful, and their character after their decease becomes the subject of unqualified eulogy. "But if those who exhibited so little evidence of piety," reasons the deceived professor, "can die thus, why then should I give myself any uneasiness? Could there be such peace where there is no piety? Could death have so little terror and be welcomed even with joy?"

9. *A false hope meets with no disturbance from the adversary.*

Why should he disturb it? It is the most effectual means of accomplishing his designs. The true Christian he will molest. If he cannot destroy his soul, he will, if possible, impair his confidence and harass his mind with fear. But the false professor has already fallen into the "snare of the devil," and it must be the policy of the great enemy to maintain that sense of security already inspired. "When a strong man armed keepeth his palace, his goods are in peace."[1]

10. There is also a *want of faithfulness in professors of religion toward each other.*

We would by no means encourage a spirit of censoriousness. "Charity thinketh no evil." It never imputes evil where no evil appears, but rather inclines us to put the most favorable construction upon the conduct of our fellow-beings. Still, charity is neither blind nor indifferent. It watches with the same solicitude over the interests of others as over our own. "In meekness," says the Apostle, "instructing those that oppose themselves; if God peradventure will give them repentance to the acknowledging of the truth; and that they may recover themselves out of the snare of the devil, who are taken captive by him at his will."[2] "Brethren, if any of you do err from the truth and one convert him, let him know that he which converteth the sinner from the error

1 Luke 11:21.
2 2 Timothy 2:25, 26.

of his way, shall save a soul from death, and shall hide a multitude of sins."[1]

Yet how sadly is this duty neglected! How often do we entertain serious doubts of the piety of those with whom we are conversant, while we have not the benevolence to express to them our fears, or to put forth any effort for their conversion! We make our remarks about their cases to others, but have no courage to speak to the individuals themselves. The tendency of this neglect is to render the confidence of the unrenewed professor more confirmed. It is indirectly, at least, healing the hurt slightly, crying peace, peace, where there is no peace.

11. *The fact that so many means have already been employed, without success, to destroy the hopes of the deceived, renders it highly probable that those hopes will be cherished to the last.*

Think of the warnings addressed to them from the Bible—think of the appeals made to them from the pulpit—think of the kind and repeated wooings of the Spirit—think of the solemn scenes of religious interest through which they may have been permitted to pass, and yet all has failed to produce any salutary impression. Truth in all its light and power has been presented; the nature of regeneration has been clearly described; and they have been urged, with melting tenderness, to "give all diligence to make their calling and election sure";

1 James 5:19, 20.

still "they hold fast deceit, they refuse to return." The hopes of others, once in the same state of deception with themselves, have been shaken and abandoned, but *their* hearts have remained unmoved, *their* security and peace undisturbed.

Chapter 5

THE REMEDY FOR
SELF-DECEPTION

Liable as self-deception is to prove permanent, it may be detected. There is a remedy for the evil, which, when applied in time, has proved effectual. That remedy is *self-examination*. The mistakes which are made in religion may all be traced to the neglect of this duty. Could men but be persuaded to search their hearts by the light of divine truth, and under the teachings of the Holy Spirit, how many hopes now firm, would at once be shaken, and be exchanged for better ones. "Let every man prove his own work."[1] "Examine yourselves whether ye be in the faith."[2]

The Bible is a plain book, and was written for minds of every order—for the unlearned as well as the learned. So clearly has it revealed the way of salvation, that even "the way-faring men, though fools, shall not err therein."[3] In a matter of such infinite

1 Galatians 6:4.
2 2 Corinthians 13:5.
3 Isaiah 35:8.

moment it might be supposed that the Holy Spirit would be explicit. It would be a reflection both on his wisdom and benevolence to say that he is not to be understood. Self-deception is not owing to any thing mysterious or ambiguous in the evidences of piety themselves, but to the want of proper attention to those evidences, and their application to our individual cases.

Men may and ought to know their true character. We may have something of the same consciousness of love to God, of repentance toward God, of faith in God, or of obedience to God, as we have of these exercises in reference to any human being. If the child may know that he loves his parents, that he respects their authority, that he trusts in their veracity, and that he is grieved for any offence committed against them, why may not the Christian know that his heart is right with God? "Lord," said Peter, "thou knowest all things; thou knowest that I love thee." Hezekiah could appeal to God that he had walked before him in truth and with a perfect heart, and had done that which was good in his sight.[1] "We know," says John, "that we have passed from death unto life, because we love the brethren."[2] "The Spirit itself beareth witness with our spirit that we are the children of God."[3]

---

1 See Isaiah 38:3.
2 1 John 3:14.
3 Romans 8:16.

1. In entering upon the investigation of our spiritual state, it is of the highest importance *that we place before us the proper standard of piety.*

The standard by which we are to try ourselves is not the suggestions of our own hearts; these are "deceitful above all things," and prone to lead us astray—not the sentiments and conduct of our fellow-men; these are often in direct opposition to the mind and will of God—not the experience of other professors; for that experience, like our own, may be spurious; and though all true Christians are born of the same Spirit, the operations of that Spirit are greatly diversified.

The proper test of piety as well as of truth is the *Bible.* This is "the man of our counsel and the guide of our life," "the law and the testimony," to which all our feelings and actions must be referred, and by which they must be tried. It is by this we are to be judged at the last day; and by this we should now prove the reality of our piety. Nothing is religion that will not bear the application of this test. Let the Bible then be our only rule of faith, of experience, and of practice.

Let the question be settled, what is the religion which God demands, and which he will finally own? Should we adopt a different standard, we may fall into the most serious mistakes, and when our state calls for alarm, it may be regarded with complacency. Our model must be, the perfect example of Him whose disciples we profess to be, and who has required us to "walk even as he walked." "If any man have not the spirit of Christ, he is none of his."

2. Not only should we fix upon a proper standard, but also *endeavor to form clear conceptions of the evidences of piety.*

Without this, we shall be liable either to the extreme of presumption or despondency. While some will cry peace when there is no peace, others, overlooking the exercises of a renewed heart, will be held in perpetual bondage to their doubts and fears. Great care should be taken to ascertain what the Scriptures insist on as *essential* to Christian character. It is by these points, and not by such as are merely circumstantial, that we are to determine the genuineness of our piety.

There are some who place great dependence upon the pungency of their convictions, the ecstasy of their joys, remarkable dreams, sudden impulses, the unexpected application of some Scripture promise, or the fact that they can refer to the particular moment and place of their supposed conversion. None of these things, however, constitute the distinguishing marks of grace. Instead therefore of directing our minds to those circumstances which may be as marked in the cases of the self-deceived as in the cases of true believers, our inquiries should relate to those traits of character which are the invariable "fruits of the Spirit," and which are common to all the subjects of his saving influence.

The following QUESTIONS from the pen of Dr. Ashbel Green are so much in point here, that we shall take the liberty of presenting them to the reader, with the earnest request that he would consider them as addressed to himself.

Have you seen yourself to be, by nature and by practice, a lost and helpless sinner? Have you not only seen the sinfulness of particular acts of transgression, but also that your heart is the seat and fountain of sin? That in you, naturally, there is no good thing? Has a view of this led you to despair of help from yourself? To see that you must be altogether indebted to Christ for salvation, and to the gracious aid of the Holy Spirit for strength and ability rightly to perform any duty?

On what has your hope of acceptance with God been founded? On your reformation? on your sorrow for your sins? on your prayers? on your tears? on your good works and religious observances? or has it been on Christ alone, as your all in all? Has Christ ever appeared very precious to you? Do you mourn that he does not appear more so? Have you sometimes felt great freedom to commit your soul to him? In doing this (if you have done it) has it been, not only to be delivered from the punishment due to your sins, but also from the power, pollution, dominion, and existence of sin in your soul?

As far as you know yourself, do you hate, and desire to be delivered from all sin—without any exception of a favorite lust? Do you pray much be delivered from sin? Do you watch against it, and against temptation to it? Do you strive against it, and in some degree get the victory over it? Have you so repented of it as to have your soul really set against it?

Have you counted the cost of following Christ or of being truly religious? That it will cut you off from vain amusement, from the indulgence of your lusts, and from a sinful conformity to the world? That it may expose you to ridicule and contempt; possibly to more serious persecution? In the view of all these things, are you willing to take up the cross and to follow Christ whithersoever he shall lead you? Is it your solemn purpose, in reliance on his grace and aid, to cleave to him, and to his cause and people, to the end of life?

Do you love holiness? Do you earnestly desire to be more and more conformed to God and to his holy law? to bear more and more the likeness of your Redeemer? Do you seek and sometimes find communion with your God and Savior?

Are you resolved, in God's strength, to endeavor conscientiously to perform your whole duty— to God, to your neighbor and to yourself?

Do you make conscience of secret prayer daily?

Do you not sometimes feel a backwardness to this duty? Do you at other times feel a great delight in it? Have you a set time, and place, and order of exercises for performing this duty?

Do you daily read a portion of the Holy Scriptures in a devout manner? Do you love to read the Bible? Do you ever perceive a sweetness in the truths of Holy Scripture? Do you find them adapted to your necessities, and see, at times, a wonderful beauty, excellence and glory in God's word? Do you make it the man of your counsel, and endeavor to have both your heart and life conformed to its doctrines and requisitions?

Have you ever attempted to covenant with God? To give yourself away to him, solemnly and irrevocably, hoping for acceptance through Christ alone; and taking God, in Christ, as the covenant God and satisfying portion of your soul?

Does the glory of God ever appear to you as the first, greatest, and best of all objects?

Do you feel a love to mankind, such as you did not formerly feel? Have you a great desire that the souls of men should be saved, by being brought to a genuine faith and trust in the Redeemer? Do you love God's people with a peculiar attachment, because they bear their Savior's image, and because they love and pursue the objects, and delight in the exercises which are most pleasing and delightful to yourself?

Do you feel it to be very important to adorn religion by a holy, exemplary, amiable, and blameless walk and conversation? Do you fear to bring a reproach on the cause of Christ? Does this appear to you extremely dreadful? Are you afraid of backsliding, and of being left to return to a state of carelessness and indifference in religion?

Do you desire and endeavor to grow in grace and in the knowledge of Christ your Savior more and more? Are you willing to sit at his feet as a little child, and to submit your reason and understanding implicitly to his teaching; imploring his Spirit to guide you into all necessary truth, to save you from all fatal errors, to enable you to receive the truth in the love of it, and to transform you, more and more, into a likeness to himself?

3. It will tend to assist you in this examination, *if your minds are directed to those objects which are calculated to elicit feeling.*

You cannot determine your state simply by looking into your hearts; you must look at truth. Every Christian grace has reference to some Bible truth, and without a distinct apprehension of that truth we cannot from the nature of the case determine the character of our exercises.

Do you wish to ascertain, for example, whether you love GOD? Then you must contemplate his *character*. Study that character as revealed in his word; and having formed scriptural views of what God is, next inquire what are the affections with which you regard him. Do you delight in his holiness, approve of his justice, acquiesce in his sovereignty, adore him for his mercy?

Do you wish to determine whether you have *repented?* Then look at *sin*—its nature, its malignancy, its ill-desert. If your heart be right, the object being presented to your mind, there will follow those affections which the character of the object is calculated to produce—self-abhorrence and contrition.

Do you wish to determine how you stand affected towards the scheme of *redemption?* Fix your attention upon that scheme as revealed in the Gospel. Reflect on the character of Christ, the design of his mission, the sufferings he endured, and the atonement he made; and with these truths before you, inquire what has been their practical influence. Do you feel the attractions of the cross and the constraining influence of a Savior's love; and abandoning every other ground of dependence, do you trust alone for salvation in Him who "was wounded for our transgressions and bruised for our iniquities?"

4. *Do not judge your state so much by your external conduct as by your internal exercises.*

We would by no means have you overlook the actions of your life. Religion is practical as well as experimental; the character of our conduct, however, is to be determined by the state of our hearts. "As a man thinketh in his heart, so is he."[1] Our judgment of others must be formed by their actions. The motives which prompt to those actions we have no power to discern. But in passing sentence upon ourselves the case is materially different. If we cannot search the hearts of our fellow-men, we may search our own; and nothing but the consciousness that we are under the influence of right affections can afford any proof of the existence of piety. The form of our actions may be right, while the principle from which they flow may be wrong. True religion consists in a "new heart and a right spirit."

5. Do not determine your state merely by *the circumstances of your supposed conversion, but by the fruit of that conversion.*

I am far from intimating that you may not be assisted in the judgment you form of your case by reverting to your first exercises. It should be a serious inquiry, what views you then entertained of yourself—of your depravity, guilt and condemnation. Carefully, too, should you determine by what means your mind became relieved—whether your hope was the result of cordial submission to Christ, or whether it originated from some other cause.

Beware, however, that you do not place undue dependence upon what might be regarded an

1 Proverbs 23:7.

extraordinary experience, while you overlook the influence which that experience has exerted upon your subsequent practice. The only evidence which some appear to furnish of their conversion, is that they were once the subjects of deep conviction, which was eventually succeeded by hope and joy. But all this may be felt while the heart is unchanged. Thousands, perhaps, have gone through this process, whose whole deportment evinces that they are yet under the dominion of sin.

> Mistaken souls! that dream of heaven,
>   And make their empty boast
> Of inward joys and sins forgiven
>   While they are slaves to lust.[1]

After all, the surest test of a genuine experience is holy living. We must "bring forth fruits meet for repentance." "Herein," says the Savior, "is my Father glorified, that ye bear much fruit; so shall ye be my disciples."[2]

6. Judge your state more by your *habitual* than by your *occasional* exercises.

Under certain circumstances an unrenewed man may be deeply excited on religious subjects, while the general tenor of his conduct may be

---

1 A quote from *Mistaken Souls that Dream of Heaven* by Isaac Watts.
2 John 15:8.

manifestly against him. Who can forbear feeling under the hand of affliction—amid the scenes of a religious revival—or under the forcible exhibition of divine truth? The genuineness of this feeling, however, must be tested by its permanency. Piety is not spasmodic or periodical, but uniform and progressive. "The path of the just is as the shining light, that shineth more and more unto the perfect day."[1] "They go from strength to strength," "always abounding in the work of the Lord."[2]

The affections of the Christian may not indeed be always alike vigorous. While there are times when he may pour out his soul in prayer with unutterable fervor, there may be times when the spirit of prayer may seem to have vanished, and his petitions be to him only like a "chattering noise." He may even woefully backslide from God, and become remiss in duty. Such, however, is not his *ordinary* state, nor is it a state in which he can remain long. His repentance will be as deep as his fall; and forgetting those things which are behind, he will press forward with renewed vigor to the immortal prize.

The late Mrs. S. Huntington has well remarked: "Character is not what a person does or is once a year, or once in half a dozen years, but what he is and does habitually. A very generous man may from mistake, or from some other cause, do what will

---

1 Proverbs 4:18.
2 1 Corinthians 15:58.

appear the excess of littleness. A very meek man may, from the pressure of perplexing circumstances, get so much off his guard as to utter things unadvisedly and improper, which he would weep tears of blood to recall. A very humble man may be placed, by the imputation of charges which he knows to be false, in a situation so irksome as to induce him to defend himself with a tone and manner entirely foreign from the general disposition and habit of his mind."

7. In determining the reality of your piety, examine not so much the *strength* of your affections as their *nature*.

Many are kept in a state of suspense, not because they believe themselves to be entirely destitute of holiness, but because their religious character is so imperfect. Now, though none ought to be satisfied with present attainments, and though no true Christian can be satisfied with the advance he has already made, still the possession of any degree of holiness is as decided proof of a state of grace as the possession of the highest degree to which the most eminent saints on earth may have arrived.

The difference between a saint and a sinner is not that the one has more holiness than the other, but that the one possesses some holiness, and the other none. As the heart of man by nature is destitute of all moral goodness, the exercise of any right affections is evidence of a gracious renewal.

While, then, it is certainly proper that we should examine the *degree* of our piety, the point now to be determined is its *reality*. The question is not whether you love God as you ought, but do you love him at all—not whether you have that measure of godly sorrow which the malignancy of sin demands, but whether your heart is really contrite and humble—not whether your faith in Christ is as strong as the Scriptures encourage you to exercise, but whether it is indeed the "faith which worketh by love"—not whether you pray with as much fervency as your wants call for and the gracious nature of God permits, but whether you have indeed "the spirit of supplication."

I am aware that this distinction is liable to abuse; still it is one of vast importance, and the man who, after having, as he supposes, ascertained that he possesses any measure of holiness, can content himself with its bare existence, and aspires not after the perfection of the Gospel, that man betrays unquestionable evidence, that, instead of loving holiness for its own sake, he regards it merely as a means to the accomplishment of some selfish end.

CONCLUSION

The writer cannot close this "labor of love" without an affectionate and earnest admonition to the reader immediately to enter upon a thorough examination of his spiritual state. The subject before you is one of pre-eminent importance, relating not merely to your welfare in time, but to your destiny for eternity. Have you a trial at court, involving your property or your reputation? You cannot rest until it be decided. Are you threatened with failure in your worldly business? with what anxiety do you examine your accounts and inquire into the state of your affairs. Are you afflicted with some dangerous disease? how seriously do you mark its symptoms and calculate on its probable result. Why then leave the greatest of all interests at stake?

If our solicitude to avoid any impending evil or to secure any anticipated good should be in proportion to their magnitude, then the salvation of the soul demands our first and principal attention.

What is the body to the soul? What is time to eternity? What is earth to heaven? What are all the evils of the present life to that undying worm, that quenchless fire which must ere long be the portion of the finally impenitent?

> Nothing is worth a thought beneath,
> But how I may escape the death
> That never, never dies!
> How make mine own election sure;
> And when I fail on earth, secure
> A mansion in the skies.[1]

Remember that the points to be settled are no less than these: Am I in a state of nature, or in a state of grace—in a state of justification, or in a state of condemnation—am I a child of God, or a child of Satan—an object of Divine favor, or an object of Divine wrath—shall I ascend to heaven, or sink to hell—shall I mingle with the ransomed around the throne, or shall I be doomed to take up my portion with the lost in outer darkness, where there is weeping and gnashing of teeth? The man who can leave questions like these unsettled, betrays a degree of moral infatuation and insensibility exceedingly alarming.

Dear Reader! whatever else you neglect, leave not this momentous interest in suspense. Earth with

---

1 A quote from *And Am I Only Born to Die?* by Charles Wesley.

all its scenes will soon vanish, and in some other portion of Jehovah's dominions you must remain in a state of conscious existence—in happiness or misery for ever. Time is your only season of probation. As you now sow, you will hereafter reap. The soul once lost, is lost irretrievably. You need not perish. The way of life is clearly marked out. If you are deceived, your deception is voluntary and criminal. If you wish to know your state, you may. Shrink not from impartial self-examination, with fervent and persevering prayer for the teachings of the Holy Spirit. It is a business upon which you must enter yourself—the writer cannot do it for you. He may furnish you with the means, but it remains for you to use them. Look to God for light. Plead with him in the language of the Psalmist, "Search me, O God, and know my heart; try me, and know my thoughts; and see if there be any wicked way in me, and lead me in the way everlasting."[1]

Should you have come to the conclusion that you are yet a stranger to grace, and are you ready in the agony of your soul to exclaim,

> My former hopes are fled,
> My terror now begins![2]

---

1 Psalm 139:23, 24.
2 A quote from *My Former Hopes Are Dead* by William Cowper.

let me beseech you—go at once to Christ. If you have never truly given yourself to him, do it now. If you have never repented, repent now. If God has shown you your danger, he also points you to your Refuge. The door of hope is yet open. You may yet be saved. Hasten to the Savior of your soul. He waits to be gracious, and has assured you that you shall "in no wise be cast out."

NOTES

NOTES

MAN'S QUESTIONS & GOD'S ANSWERS

Am I accountable to God?
Each of us will give an account of himself to God. ROMANS 14:12 (NIV).

Has God seen all my ways?
Everything is uncovered and laid bare before the eyes of him to whom we must give account. HEBREWS 4:13 (NIV).

Does he charge me with sin?
But the Scripture declares that the whole world is a prisoner of sin. GALATIANS 3:22 (NIV).
All have sinned and fall short of the glory of God. ROMANS 3:23 (NIV).

Will he punish sin?
The soul who sins is the one who will die. EZEKIEL 18:4 (NIV).
For the wages of sin is death, but the gift of God is eternal life in Christ Jesus our Lord. ROMANS 6:23 (NIV).

Must I perish?
He is patient with you, not wanting anyone to perish, but everyone to come to repentance. 2 PETER 3:9 (NIV).

How can I escape?
Believe in the Lord Jesus, and you will be saved. ACTS 16:31 (NIV).

Is he able to save me?
Therefore he is able to save completely those who come to God through him. HEBREWS 7:25 (NIV).

Is he willing?
Christ Jesus came into the world to save sinners. 1 TIMOTHY 1:15 (NIV).

Am I saved on believing?
Whoever believes in the Son has eternal life, but whoever rejects the Son will not see life, for God's wrath remains on him. JOHN 3:36 (NIV).

Can I be saved now?
Now is the time of God's favor, now is the day of salvation. 2 CORINTHIANS 6:2 (NIV).

As I am?
Whoever comes to me I will never drive away. JOHN 6:37 (NIV).

Shall I not fall away?
Him who is able to keep you from falling. JUDE 1:24 (NIV).

If saved, how should I live?
Those who live should no longer live for themselves but for him who died for them and was raised again. 2 CORINTHIANS 5:15 (NIV).

What about death and eternity?
I am going there to prepare a place for you. I will come back and take you to be with me that you also may be where I am. JOHN 14:2-3 (NIV).

www.ingramcontent.com/pod-product-compliance
Lightning Source LLC
Chambersburg PA
CBHW020602030426
42337CB00013B/1178